Clara and the Missing Chickens: A Mystery in the Coop

This is a work of fiction. Names, characters, businesses, organizations, places, events, and incidents either are the product of the author's imagination or are used fictitiously. Any resemblance to actual persons, living or dead, events, or locales is entirely coincidental.

The following trademarked terms are mentioned in this book: Mohamed El Afia. The use of these trademarks does not indicate an endorsement of this work by the trademark owners. The trademarks are used in a purely descriptive sense and all trademark rights remain with the trademark owner.

Cover design by el Emma afia.

This book was typeset in Emma afia.

First edition, 2023.

Published by Emma Afia.

Chapter 1: The Disappearance

- Clara discovers that several chickens are missing from the coop
- She investigates the coop and finds some clues, including feathers and footprints
- Clara decides to solve the mystery and find out what happened to the chickens

Chapter 2: Suspects and Clues

- Clara interviews various suspects, including the mischievous fox and a mysterious neighbor
- She finds more clues, including a torn piece of cloth and a strange smell near the coop
- Clara begins to piece together the clues and develop some theories about what happened

Chapter 3: Dead Ends and New Leads

- Clara hits some dead ends in her investigation and becomes discouraged
- She receives some unexpected help from a friend who suggests a new lead
- Clara follows the lead and discovers some surprising information that changes everything

Chapter 4: Showdown

- Clara confronts the culprit and demands an explanation
- The culprit reveals their motive and Clara realizes the full extent of the situation
- Clara comes up with a plan to right the wrongs and restore the missing chickens to their rightful place

Chapter 5: Resolution

- Clara's plan works and the missing chickens are returned to the coop
- Clara and her family celebrate their success and reflect on what they've learned
- Clara realizes that the experience has taught her the importance of responsibility, problem-solving, and being a good steward of the animals and the environment.

Chapter 1: The Disappearance

Clara woke up early one morning and headed towards the chicken coop as she did every day. She loved spending time with her chickens, but as she approached the coop, she noticed that something was off. Several chickens were missing. Clara was surprised and puzzled. She checked around the coop and found some clues: scattered feathers on the ground and some unusual footprints

Clara knew that something was wrong and decided to investigate. She began to ask around, but no one had seen anything suspicious. Clara was determined to get to the bottom of this and find out what happened to her beloved chickens. She set out to investigate the area around the coop, hoping to find some more clues to solve the mystery.

Chapter 2: Suspects and Clues

Clara's investigation leads her to interview various suspects, including the mischievous fox and a mysterious neighbor. The fox had a reputation for being a chicken thief, and Clara was suspicious of him. However, the neighbor seemed friendly and harmless, and Clara didn't think he could be involved in the disappearance.

As Clara searched for more clues, she discovered a torn piece of cloth and a strange smell near the coop. The cloth didn't belong to anyone on the farm, and the smell was unfamiliar. Clara began to suspect that someone else might be responsible for the missing chickens.

With these new clues in hand, Clara started to develop some theories about what might have happened. She spent hours poring over the evidence, trying to make sense of it all. But the more she investigated, the more confused she became. The case seemed to be getting more complicated by the minute.

Chapter 3: Dead Ends and New Leads

Clara hits some dead ends in her investigation, and she becomes discouraged. She starts to think that she might not be able to solve the mystery. However, just when Clara was about to give up, she received some unexpected help from a friend who suggested a new lead.

Clara followed her friend's advice and discovered a clue that led her to an abandoned shed on the outskirts of the farm. Inside the shed, she found some evidence that shed light on the mystery. Clara felt a renewed sense of hope and determination. She knew that she was getting closer to solving the case.

As Clara continued her investigation, she discovered some surprising information that changed everything. She had been looking in the wrong direction all along. The culprit was someone she never suspected, and the motive was something she never would have guessed.

With this new information, Clara knew that it was time to confront the culprit and demand an explanation. She had come too far to give up now. She was determined to get to the bottom of the mystery, no matter what it took.

Chapter 4: Showdown

Clara confronts the culprit and demands an explanation. The culprit initially denies everything, but Clara has evidence that proves their guilt. The culprit finally confesses and reveals their motive. Clara is shocked by what she hears.

The culprit explains that they had taken the chickens to sell them at the market to make some quick money. They didn't think anyone would notice, and they were desperate for cash. Clara is angry and disappointed. She had trusted this person and never imagined they could do something so dishonest.

Clara decides to come up with a plan to right the wrongs and restore the missing chickens to their rightful place. She knows that it won't be easy, but she is determined to make things right. With the help of her family and friends, Clara sets out to make things right and fix the damage that was done.

In the end, Clara's plan works, and the missing chickens are returned to the coop. Clara and her family celebrate their success and reflect on what they've learned. Clara realizes that the experience has taught her the importance of responsibility, problem-solving, and being a good steward of the animals and the environment. She also learns the importance of forgiveness and the power of second chances

Chapter 5: Resolution

In the aftermath of the mystery, Clara and her family reflect on what they've learned. They talk about the importance of taking care of the animals on their farm and being good stewards of the environment. They also talk about the importance of honesty, responsibility, and forgiveness.

Clara and her family decide to take extra precautions to make sure that something like this never happens again. They install better security around the coop and make sure that all of the animals are accounted for each day.

Clara also decides to share her experience with others. She talks to her friends and neighbors about what happened and encourages them to be more vigilant and responsible when it comes to taking care of their animals. She hopes that her story will inspire others to be more mindful and responsible in their own lives.

In the end, Clara feels a sense of satisfaction and accomplishment. She has solved the mystery and learned some valuable lessons along the way. She knows that she will never forget this experience and that it will shape the person she becomes in the future.

The End

Cover design by el Emma afia.

This book was typeset in Emma afia.

First edition, 2023.

Published by Emma Afia.

Made in the USA
Monee, IL
17 June 2023

36033817R10015